Where We Like to Go

Peter Sloan and Sheryl Sloan

The Circus

We like to go to the circus.

The circus is a place where we can see people and animals do many clever things.

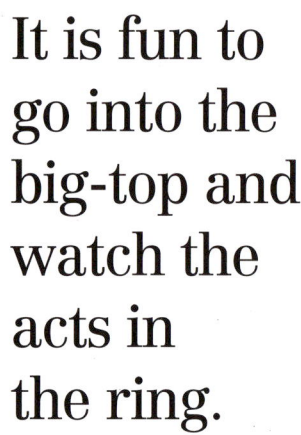

It is fun to go into the big-top and watch the acts in the ring.

The trapeze act is exciting. Trapeze artists hang upside down from high up in the air. They catch each other as they leap from the swinging bars.

The clowns are always funny. They chase each other and do tricks on one another.

Animal tamers stand in a cage with the lions and tigers and get them to do tricks. It is very dangerous.

We like to watch the balancing and juggling acts.

The Museum

We like to go to the museum.

There are all sorts of displays to see. Some displays show things that people used long ago such as clay pots, coins or clothes.

Other displays show the skeletons of animals.

We like to see the big dinosaur skeletons.

We like to see the animal hall with all the stuffed animals standing together.

We like to see the history hall. We can see the things people used over a hundred years ago.

In the museum there are things to do and touch. We can sit in an old coach or touch the organs inside a model of a human body.

The Zoo

We like to go to the zoo.

At the zoo there are our favourite animals to see and new animal babies to look at.

Sometimes we can see rare animals from other zoos.

At the zoo we like to watch the big cats being fed.

At the zoo we like to watch the elephants bathe.

At the zoo we watch the monkeys climbing and playing in the trees.

In the reptile house at the zoo we can see the snakes and lizards.

The Farm

We like to go to the farm.

Most farms have animals. Even big farms which grow crops like wheat or corn have some animals.

They may have cows, sheep, goats, or even hens.

On some farms there are big machines for working on the land and for gathering crops.

In the morning and evening cows on dairy farms are brought to the milking shed to be milked.

On sheep farms the sheep are brought into the shearing shed to have their wool shorn off.

Horses on farms can be good to ride and we can ride them for fun.

The Fair

We like to go to the fair. It is an exciting place with flashing lights and loud music.

At the fair there are many families having fun together. There is always something new to do or to see.

There are colourful and exciting parades to see at the fair.

The animal parades and horse events are interesting to watch.

There are many rides to go on, like the Big Wheel and Merry-go-rounds.

We can play games and try to win prizes from the stalls.

The Park

We like to go to the park.

A good park is a safe place for parents to take their children.

At the park we can play with other children.

The park is a good place to have a picnic.

There are swings and slides to have fun on at the park.

There are grassy places to run and play games on.

There are places for skating and rollerblading.

The Library

We like to go to the library.

The librarians at the library show us what to do and where to find the things that we want.

Sometimes the library has special activities for children during school holidays.

At the library we can get the latest books to read. We can look at the displays and borrow videos.

At the library we can listen to people read stories.

At the library we can listen to music and take out the CDs.

At the library we can play with the construction sets.

In this book there are many good places for children to go.

Which one did you like the best?

When we go to these places we should always obey the rules and stay with our teachers or parents.